GOLF: LIFE ON THE COURSE

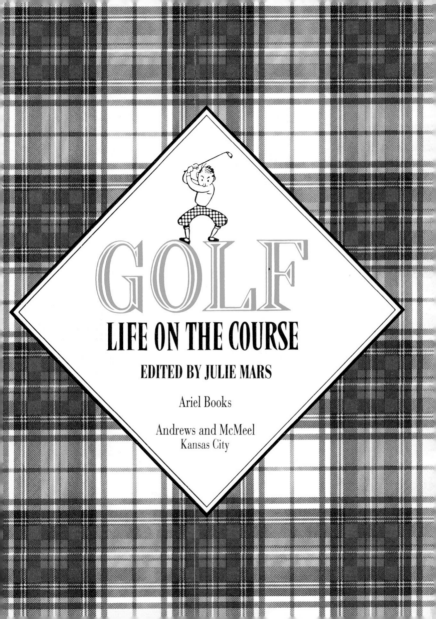

GOLF
LIFE ON THE COURSE

EDITED BY JULIE MARS

Ariel Books

Andrews and McMeel
Kansas City

ISBN: 0-8362-4718-3
Library of Congress Catalog Card Number: 94-71138

The text of this book was set in Bauer Bodoni Condensed
by Harry Chester Inc., New York City.

Designed by Michael Mendelsohn

CONTENTS

INTRODUCTION

GOLF: SPORT, LIFESTYLE, OR OBSESSION?

Why do people love this game? Ask golfers and the answers will range from "It's the fresh air and the exercise" to, in the words of amateur champ Walter Travis, "Golf is something more than a game. It is a religion." Perhaps this gives us a clue to the amazing popularity of golf: it can be anything you want it to be, from a casual pastime to a deep personal obsession. From its humble beginnings as a ragtag game played with crude sticks and a feather-stuffed ball, golf has become progressively more organized, more accessible, and more sophisticated—and it has spread like wildfire across the globe.

Golf is now played on every continent in the world (except Antarctica). In the United States alone, about twenty million players flock to over 8,500 courses every year. You can start when you're eight (or younger) and play until you're seventy-five (or even older). You can tee off in an extinct volcano in Bali or at 14,335 feet above sea level on Peru's Morocacha Mountain.

There are as many good reasons to play golf as there are golfers, but one thing is certain: After more than five and a half centuries, "golfitis" is thriving. It can strike anyone. And once the love of the game gets in your blood, the world may never look exactly the same to you again.

IT'S HOW YOU PLAY THE GAME

ADVICE FROM THE EXPERTS

Golfers will do anything to improve their swings—and ultimately their scores. Whether amateur golfers seek their own inner games or the advice of a golf guru, one thing is certain: they're looking for a "swing key" to the magical game of golf. Here are some individual opinions and some popular wisdom on just how to play this game:

Let your hands take it away, laddie, and feel the grass.

—Scottish wisdom on the game

There is one categorical imperative, "Hit the Ball," but there are no minor absolutes.

—Sir Walter Simpson

Keep on hitting it straight until the wee ball goes in the hole.

—James Braid

Too many golfers grip the club at address like they were trying to choke a prairie coyote to death.

—Curt Wilson

To control his own ball, all alone without help or hindrance, the golfer must first and last control himself. At each stroke, the ball becomes a vital extension, an image of one's innermost self.

—John Stuart Martin

Only one golfer in a thousand grips the club lightly enough.

—Johnny Miller

Golf is a hands game.

—Henry Cotton

Golf is played with the arms.

—Sam Snead

When I play my best, I feel I'm playing with my legs
and feet.

—Sam Snead

Imagine the ball has little legs, and chop them off.

—Henry Cotton

When I want a long ball, I spin my hips faster.

—Jack Nicklaus

Concentrate on hitting *the green*. The cup will come
to you.

—Cary Middlecoff

Just knock hell out of it with your right hand.

—Tommy Armour

Swing hard in case you hit it.

—Dan Marino

Let the club swing itself through. Help it on all you can but do not you begin to hit with it. Let it do its work itself and it will do it well. Interfere with it, and it will be quite adequately revenged.

—Horace Hutchinson

Don't hurry, don't worry. . . be sure to stop and smell the flowers.

—Walter Hagen

RULES OF THE LINKS

In 1754, the twenty-two noblemen and gentlemen of the Society of St. Andrews, Scotland—now called the Royal and Ancient Golf Club of St. Andrews—formally declared the "Articles and Laws in Playing the Golf." These thirteen original rules, with minor variations, have governed the game ever since. A couple of excerpts indicate some of the difficulties of the game at the time:

> If a ball is stop'd by any person, horse, dog, or anything else, the ball so stop'd must be played where it lyes.

> If you draw your club in order to strike and proceed so far with your stroke as to be bringing down your club, if then your club should break in any way, it is to be accounted a stroke.

Golfers these days do not have to contend with roving livestock on the courses, and advances in club-manufacturing technology pretty much guarantee clubs won't break in your hands—unless you imitate Tommy Bolt, whose club-breaking antics are legendary.

As a sport, golf demands strength, precision, and endurance. However, as a way of life, it requires careful consideration of others, strict adherence to a code of honor, and superior sportsmanship. These requirements were not ignored by the Royal and Ancient Golf Club. Rule seven states, "At holing you are to play your ball honestly for the hole, and not to play upon your adversary's ball, not lying in your way to the hole."

As many golfers are quick to point out, a sense of humor doesn't hurt either. Here are some immortal words from golfers on the subject of rules and etiquette:

Golf is the only game in which a precise knowledge of the rules can earn one a reputation for bad sportsmanship.

—Patrick Campbell

There are two basic rules which should never be broken. Be subtle. And don't, for God's sake, try to do business with anyone who's having a bad game.

—William Davis

Golf appeals to the idiot in us and the child. What child does not grasp the pleasure principle of miniature golf? Just how childlike golf players become is proven by their frequent inability to count past five.

—John Updike

It's good sportsmanship to not pick up lost golf balls while they are still rolling.

—Mark Twain

At first a golfer excuses a dismal performance by claiming bad lies. With experience, he covers up with better ones.

—P. Brown

Never bet with anyone you meet on the first tee who has a deep suntan, a 1-iron in his bag, and squinty eyes.

—David Marr

If you are going to throw a club, it is important to throw it ahead of you, down the fairway, so you don't waste energy going back to pick it up.

—Tommy Bolt

If your adversary is badly bunkered, there is no rule against your standing over him and counting his strokes aloud, with increasing gusto as their number mounts up; but it will be a wise precaution to arm yourself with the niblick before doing so, so as to meet him on equal terms.

—Horace Hutchinson

If you call on God to improve the results of a shot while it is still in motion, you are using "an outside agency" and subject to appropriate penalties under the rules of golf.

—Henry Longhurst

GOLF FACTS

When it comes to golf, every player has a theory . . . and each one has a great story to tell. It might even be said it's part of a golfer's responsibilties as a player to offer a little advice, philosophy, or inspiration. Each insight into the game or story of a miraculous hole in one adds to golf's overall mystique.

Tom Morris, Jr., in the 1868 Open Championship at Prestwick, made the first recorded hole in one.

Chances of making a hole in one if you're not a pro: 1:12,600.

The oldest person in the world to ace was Otto Bucher. He was ninety-nine when he scored a hole in one in 1985. And two six-year-olds—Tommy Moore (1968) and Brittny Andreas (1991)—beat the odds, too.

No one knows *why* the warning shout of "Fore!" is used all over the world, but we do know the first person to shout it was a caddie named Herd, in 1854. One speculation is that it's a shortened version of "Beware before!"—which is shouted by the British army artillery as a warning to the infantry in front of them. The infantry would lie down to let the cannonballs pass over their heads. Golfers are thus warned by fellow players that ducking might be a good idea.

The human traffic is so heavy on the Fukuoka Golf Course in Japan that stop-and-go lights have been placed at three holes.

The Nyanza Club in British East Africa (1950) allowed a player another ball, without penalty, if the first landed too near a crocodile or a hippopotamus.

One unlucky golfer named D. J. Bayly MacArthur attempted to play out of a sand trap in Australia—and he soon learned it was quicksand. No one came along to help him until he had sunk up to his armpits.

Another unlucky golfer, named McFarland, was convicted of manslaughter in 1939. He said, "I swung my club in disgust too forcibly." It flew out of his hands—and killed his caddie.

When golf balls were made of leather and stuffed by hand with feathers, a good worker could produce only four balls a day.

When the unexpected or unusual happens, golfers call it the "rub of the green," meaning "tough luck" or "those are the breaks." The phrase was used in the code of the Royal and Ancient Golf Club of 1812 in rule nine: "Whatever happens to a ball by accident must be reckoned a rub of the green."

The finest wood clubs are made of a type of ebony called persimmon, with the grain carefully matched for beauty and craftsmanship. Not-so-fine woods made of metal are called "Pittsburgh persimmon."

The wooden tee was invented in 1920 by Dr. William Lowell, a Boston dentist and golfer. Dr. Lowell wanted to protect his hands from becoming scratched. Golfers previously would make a small pile of sand or dirt for the ball.

Ever wonder why pros look up before selecting a club and down before putting? Looking up at the tops of trees helps them judge the wind speed and direction that will influence a shot. When they look down, they're probably checking the condition of the green and the cup—water that collects at the edge of the green will indicate slopes and breaks in the green that are difficult to see, while a cup with a worn rim or grass that is clipped closely on one side will also affect their shot.

Pro golfers will dig their feet into the sand in a bunker for two reasons: to anchor themselves for the shot and to test the condition of the sand. Rules forbid any other way of testing the consistency of the sand.

GOLF QUIPS AND QUOTES

Real golfers don't cry when they line up their fourth putt.

—Karen Hurwitz

The hardest shot is a mashie at ninety yards from the green, where the ball has to be played against an oak tree, bounces back into a sand trap, hits a stone, bounces on the green and then rolls into the cup. That shot is so difficult I have only made it once.

—Zeppo Marx

A game in which a ball one-and-a-half inches in diameter is placed on a ball eight thousand miles in diameter. The object is to hit the small ball but not the larger.

—John Cunningham

I know I'm getting better at golf because I'm hitting fewer spectators.

—Gerald Ford

If I swung a gavel the way I swung that golf club, the nation would be in a helluva mess.

—Tip O'Neill

It took me seventeen years to get three thousand hits in baseball. I did it in one afternoon on the golf course.

—Hank Aaron

To get an elementary grasp of the game of golf, a human must learn, by endless practice, a continuous and subtle series of highly unnatural movements, involving about sixty-four muscles, that result in a seemingly natural swing, taking all of two seconds to begin and end.

—Alistair Cooke

The more I practice, the luckier I get.

—Gary Player

If every golfer in the world, male and female, were laid end to end, I, for one, would leave them there.

—Mark Parkinson,
president, Anti-Golf Society

The difference between golf and government is that in golf you can't improve your lie.

—George Doukmejian

If you watch a game, it's fun. If you play it, it's recreation. If you work at it, it's golf.

—Bob Hope

On the golf course, a man may be the dogged victim of inexorable fate, be struck down by an appalling stroke of tragedy, become the hero of unbelievable melodrama, or the clown in a side-splitting comedy.

—Bobby Jones

Have you ever noticed what golf spells backwards?

—Al Boliska

Golf is more exacting than racing, cards, speculation, or matrimony. In almost all other games you pit yourself against a mortal foe; in golf it is yourself against the world: no human being stays your progress as you drive your ball over the face of the globe.

—Arnold Haultain

The truly great things happen when a genius is alone. This is true especially among golfers.

—J. R. Coulson

Golf and sex are about the only things you can enjoy without being good at it.

—Jimmy Demaret

When I look on my life and try to decide out of what I have got most actual pleasure, I have no doubt at all in saying that I have got more out of golf than anything else.

—Lord Brabazon

Excessive golfing dwarfs the intellect. Nor is this to be wondered at when we consider that the more fatuously vacant the mind is, the better for play. It has been observed that absolute idiots play the steadiest.

—Sir Walter Simpson

Golf is in the interest of good health and good manners. It promotes self-restraint and affords a chance to play the man and act the gentleman.

—William Howard Taft

Golf is typical capitalist lunacy.

—George Bernard Shaw

I don't trust doctors. They are like golfers. Every one has a different answer to your problem.

—Severiano Ballesteros

It is a test of temper, a trial of honour, a revealer of character. It means going into God's out-of-doors, getting close to nature, fresh air and exercise, a sweeping of mental cobwebs, and a genuine relaxation of tired tissues.

—David Forgan

My favourite shots are the practice swing and the conceded putt. The rest can never be mastered.

—Lord Robertson

Beyond the fact that it is a limitless arena for the full play of human nature, there is no sure accounting for golf's fascination. . . . Perhaps it is nothing more than the best game man has ever devised.

—Herbert Warren Wind

I guess there is nothing that will get your mind off everything like golf. I have never been depressed enough to take up the game but they say you get so sore at yourself you forget to hate your enemies.

—Will Rogers

Golf is a science, the study of a lifetime, in which you can exhaust yourself but never your subject.

—David Forgan

Golf puts a man's character on the anvil and his richest qualities—patience, poise, restraint—to the flame.

—Billy Casper

In golf, humiliations are the essence of the game.

—Alistair Cooke

Golf is 20 percent mechanics and technique. The other 80 percent is philosophy, humor, tragedy, romance, melodrama, companionship, camaraderie, cussedness, and conversation.

—Grantland Rice

Give me a man with big hands and big feet and no brains and I'll make a golfer out of him.

—Walter Hagen

The better you putt, the bolder you play.

—Don January

Never break your putter and your driver in the same round or you're dead.

—Tommy Bolt

The only way of really finding out a man's true character is to play golf with him. In no other walk of life does the cloven hoof so quickly display itself.

—P. G. Wodehouse

Be funny on a golf course? Do I kid my best friend's mother about her heart condition?

—Phil Silvers

The best stroked putt in a lifetime does not bring the aesthetic satisfaction of a perfectly hit wood or iron shot. There is nothing to match the whoosh and soar, the almost magical flight of a beautifully hit drive or 5-iron.

—Al Barkow

Golfers find it a very trying matter to turn at the waist, more particularly if they have a lot of waist to turn.

—Harry Vardon

I never pray on a golf course. Actually, the Lord answers my prayers everywhere except on the course.

—Billy Graham

Miss a putt for two thousand dollars? Not likely!

—Walter Hagen

Golf is assuredly a mystifying game. It would seem that if a person has hit a golf ball correctly a thousand times, he should be able to duplicate the performance at will. But such is certainly not the case.

—Bobby Jones

The only time I talk on a golf course is to my caddie. And then only to complain when he gives me the wrong club.

—Severiano Ballesteros

What other people may find in poetry, I find in the flight of a good drive.

—Arnold Palmer

FAMOUS GOLF COURSES

What makes a good golf course? Pros, weekenders, and armchair enthusiasts all agree that, although any number of factors can diminish a course's appeal, the best courses share a few simple but important traits. On the most basic level, the grass should be well kept and of good quality, with effective drainage so the fairways and greens don't get soggy and water doesn't collect in puddles. Next, the course should fit into the natural environment . . . because it has been carefully carved from it. And last, each hole should be placed in such a way that all the players, beginners as well as pros, face an exciting, pleasant challenge when they step up to the tee. Each hole should test the players' physical and mental stamina, their judgment—and possibly their luck. Hazards are an important part of the design—and the challenge.

A good game of golf can be had on thousands of courses, yet a look at a few world-class courses makes every golfer dream.

The Old Course at St. Andrews, Scotland: These are probably the most famous links on earth—golf has been played here continuously for at least four centuries. Known for its incredible collection of natural hazards (pits, for example, where long ago people dug for shells) and the whimsical winds from the sea, St. Andrews is the final destination for many a golf pilgrim. Since 1754, when the previously mentioned twenty-two gentlemen and noblemen of St. Andrews gathered to compete for a silver club, all the greats of golf have loved—and sometimes cursed—this course. It consists of nine holes out, toward the Eden estuary, and the same nine holes back. Length: 6,960 yards. Par 72.

Ballybunion, Ireland: On the rugged and spectacular southwest coast in Kerry, this course is known for its sand dunes covered with long grass as well as its uphill, downhill, and sidehill lies. Ballybunion is laden with punitive bunkers that have caused great grief and regret to many a golfer. Originally founded in 1893, it was forced to close five years later due to serious money woes, but it reopened in 1906. Erosion, which threatened the course in the 1970s, was arrested through the efforts of Jack Harrigan's "Friends of Ballybunion" organization. Length: 6,542 yards. Par 71.

Shinnecock Hills, **New York:** Located in Southampton on eastern Long Island, this was completed in 1892, the first 18-hole course in America. Similar in design and location to the Scottish links on which the designer, Willie Dunn, had played, Shinnecock Hills was built almost entirely by hand by 150 Native Americans from the Shinnecock Reservation. Many Indian artifacts have been discovered there among the bunkers. Like Ballybunion, the reedy grass and sandy hills, along with the strong prevailing ocean winds, create a challenging ambience for any golfer. Length: 6,697 yards. Par 70.

Pinehurst, **North Carolina:** Originally conceived as a winter getaway for golfing New Englanders, Pinehurst was designed by the great golf architect Donald Ross, who called it "the fairest test of champions [he] had ever designed." With water hazards limited to the sixteenth hole, the course is nestled among tall pine trees that provide subtle encouragement for staying on the fairway. The pine needles form an interesting natural hazard, as do the mounds guarding the greens. Length: 7,028 yards. Par 71.

Pebble Beach, **California:** Built along the magnificent Carmel coast, Pebble Beach is renowned for its difficult though thrilling series of seaside holes. Players face blind tee-offs placed at the edge of cliffs and fight wind, downhill fairway slopes, and even a natural promontory where the waves crash over the rocks. This exhilarating course presents a formidable challenge each and every step of the way. Length: 6,815 yards. Par 72.

COURSE COMMENTS

I'd like to see the fairways more narrow. Then everybody would have to play from the rough, not just me.

—Severiano Ballesteros

The behaviour etiquette for greenside bunkers should go into reverse. Players should be forbidden to smooth them in any way. The bunker should be the fearful place it once was, not the perfect surface from which a pro expects to float his ball out stone dead, something he doesn't expect when chipping.

—Michael Hobbs

The grounds on which golf is played are called links, being the barren sandy soil from which the sea has retired in recent geological times. In their natural state links are covered with long, rank bent grass and gorse.

Links are too barren for cultivation: but sheep, rabbits, geese and professionals pick up a precarious livelihood on them.

—Sir Walter Simpson

If a man is to get into a hazard let it be a bad one. Let the lies within your hazard be as bad as you please—the worse the better. So leave your whins without any pruning or thinning and if the bottom of your sand bunker gets smooth-beaten, howk it up.

—Horace Hutchinson

Even in defeat, the scenic surroundings at Pebble Beach were absolutely dazzling, the dream of an artist who had been drinking gin and sobering up on absinthe. It is too extravagantly decorated not to be a painting. Snow-white sand in the bunkers; vividly green turf, coccusbent green. The Bay of Naples is no more lovely and not as blue as the inlet, Carmel Bay, along which the course is built.

—O. B. Keeler

At Jinga there is both hotel and golf course. The latter is, I believe, the only course in the world which posts a special rule that the player may remove his ball from hippopotamus footprints.

—Evelyn Waugh